Contents

Some words are shown in bold, **like this**. You can find out what they mean by looking in the glossary.

LET'S LOOK AT
British animals!

Britain is famous for its wildlife. There are many places to spot animals of all types, from beautiful beaches to busy cities. Read on to find out more about these **habitats** and meet the animals that live in them!

WOODLANDS

Woodlands are areas of land covered with tall trees. Lots of different animals, such as the Scottish wildcat, live in woodland. The wildcat is one of Britain's largest land **predators**.

wildcat

Let's Look at...

Animals

OF THE
BRITISH ISLES

Lucy Beevor

raintree

a Capstone company — publishers for children

Raintree is an imprint of Capstone Global Library Limited, a company incorporated in England and Wales having its registered office at 264 Banbury Road, Oxford, OX2 7DY – Registered company number: 6695582

www.raintree.co.uk
myorders@raintree.co.uk
Text © Capstone Global Library Limited 2019
The moral rights of the proprietor have been asserted.

Edited by Clare Lewis
Designed by Cynthia Della-Rovere
Original illustrations © Capstone Global Library Limited 2018
Picture research by Jo Miller
Production by Tori Abraham
Originated by Capstone Global Library Ltd
Printed and bound in India

ISBN 978 1 4747 6388 2 (hardback)
22 21 20 19 18
10 9 8 7 6 5 4 3 2 1

ISBN 978 1 4747 6392 9 (paperback)
23 22 21 20 19
10 9 8 7 6 5 4 3 2 1

British Library Cataloguing in Publication Data
A full catalogue record for this book is available from the British Library.

Acknowledgements
We would like to thank the following for permission to reproduce photographs: We would like to thank the following for permission to reproduce photographs: Alamy: BIOSPHOTO/Frederic Desmette, 11 Bottom, blickwinkel/Hecker, 21 Top, Glyn Thomas, 28 BL, jack perks, 20 TR, Jordon Sharp, 16 Top, PAUL R. STERRY, 15 BL, 15 MB, Scubazoo, 17 Top; Dreamstime: Tramper2, 9 TR; Getty Images: Arterra/UIG, 12 MR; Minden Pictures: Denis Bringard, 21 MB, Jane Burton, 21 BL, Jelger Herder, 21 BR; Shutterstock: Alexander Raths, 29 BL, Andrew Balcombe, 11 Middle, Andrew Roland, 6 Middle, Ant Cooper, 26 Top, aquapix, 5 TM, Bright, 10 Bottom, chris froome, 9 TL, Chris Moody, 7 MR, Christian Schoissingeyer, 2, 12 BL, Coatesy, 8 Right, colin robert varndell, 5 BR, Dirk Ercken, 20 BR, DJTaylor, 5 BL, Eddie J. Rodriquez, 4 Top, Erni, 16 BR, Ervin Monn, 7 TR, ESK Imagery, 24 BL, Gail Johnson, 13 Middle, Grant M Henderson, 24 TR, Heiko Kiera, 12 TR, Helen Hotson, 5 TL, 7 TL, Henrik Larsson, 27 TR, Hugh Lansdown, 28 TL, irin-k, 27 BL, Jakinnboaz, 19 Bottom, James Pearce, 5 MB, JASON STEEL, 7 BL, Jiri Prochazka, 16 BL, Karel Gallas, 27 BR, Kletr, Cover TL, 22 BL, lanaid12, 25 BR, Lisa S., 29 BR, Lynsey Allan, 25 Left, Maciej Olszewski, 26 Middle, Mantonature, 19 Top, Marco Maggesi, 18 Top, Mark Bridger, 4 Bottom, Mark Caunt, 22 Top, Mark Medcalf, 9 BL, Martin Fowler, 19 Middle, 28 TR, MF Photo, 14, Michal Ninger, 1, 7 ML, Migel, 24 BR, Mirko Graulo, Cover Bottom, Miroslav Hlavko, Cover Back, 10 TR, MP cz, 24 TL, N Mrtgh, 27 TL, nnnnae, Design Element, Patila, 29 Middle, Peter Turner Photography, 17 Bottom, Peter Wey, 32, Philip Bird LRPS CPAGB, 6 Bottom, Podolnaya Elena, 23 BR, Redai Paul Stefan, 15 BR, Richard Bowden, 11 Top, Rostislav Stefanek, 23 BL, 23 TR, Rudmer Zwerver, 3, 8 Left, 9 BR, 10 TL, 13 Top, 29 TR, Sakurra, 22 BR, Sandra Standbridge, Cover TR, 5 TR, snapgalleria, 28 BR, Stephan Morris, 12 BR, Sue Berry, 6 Top, Susana_Martins, 25 MR, taviphoto, Cover Middle, Tory Kallman, 13 Bottom, Uve Kirsch, 26 Bottom, Valentina Moraru, 15 TR, 18 Bottom, Vicky Jirayu, 7 BR, Vladimir Wrangel, 23 TL, 25 TR, WitR, 20 Left, Wolfgang Simlinger, 15 TL.

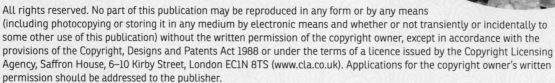

OCEANS AND SEAS

The oceans and seas around Britain are brimming with sea life. Electric rays are some of Britain's strangest sea fish. They make an electric shock to **stun** both their **prey** and their predators.

natterjack toad

BEACHES

Beaches are sandy areas by the sea. Many small animals live here. Natterjack toads make their homes in **sand dunes**.

electric ray

raft spider

BOGS

Bogs are areas of wet, muddy ground. Many small, light animals **thrive** in bogs. The raft spider skates across the bog water.

MOUNTAINS

The mountain hare lives high up in the snowy mountains of Scotland. In winter its fur changes colour, from brown to white. This makes it harder for **predators** to spot the hare in the snow.

mountain hare

Migration

Not all animals live in Britain all year round. Some visit us for part of the year. This is called migration. Thousands of painted-lady butterflies fly to Britain to **breed** every summer. When the chilly autumn weather arrives, the butterflies return to their much warmer home in southern Europe.

perch

bumblebee

RIVERS AND CANALS

Many types of fish **thrive** in Britain's rivers, streams and canals. The perch can grow up to 60 centimetres long in canals.

GRASSLANDS

Colourful wildflowers grow in grasslands. The flowers attract thousands of minibeasts, such as bumblebees.

GARDENS

Many animals visit British gardens during the day and at night. The grass snake is Britain's largest snake. It sometimes slithers into gardens to look for food. But don't worry, the grass snake is completely harmless.

grass snake

Mammals

Scientists have divided animals into groups. The groups are made up of animals that are alike in important ways.

Mammals have hair. They are warm-blooded and have a **backbone**. There are over 100 types of mammal in the UK. Britain's smallest mammal is the pygmy shrew. Our biggest land mammal is the red deer stag. Humans are mammals too!

RABBITS

Rabbits are a common sight in Britain. You may see them in fields or on grass by the side of the road. Rabbits live in large groups. They dig **burrows** and long tunnels underground.

HEDGEHOGS

Hedgehogs live in parks and gardens. They eat slugs and worms. Hedgehogs have spines on their backs. If they are frightened, they can roll into a prickly ball for protection.

SQUIRRELS

Grey squirrels are common in Britain. Red squirrels are more rare. Squirrels live in trees. They have nests called dreys. Squirrels are very good at leaping from tree to tree.

grey squirrel

red squirrel

MOLES

You can often see molehills in fields and gardens. These are the piles of earth left where moles have been digging their underground tunnels. Moles trap worms and insects in their tunnels. They need to eat around 20 worms a day to survive!

MICE

Wood mice live in woods, fields and hedgerows. They are **nocturnal**. Mice have many **predators**, including owls, foxes, weasels and stoats. Mice have lots of babies. A female can have up to 60 young in one year!

wood mouse

SHREWS

Shrews are smaller than mice. They have tiny eyes and long noses.

pygmy shrew

They dash about looking through old leaves, bark and grass for worms, spiders and insects to eat. Pygmy shrews are the smallest shrews. They usually hide away from humans. You might be able to hear their high squeaks if they are fighting nearby!

DORMICE

Dormice are tiny mammals. They have hairy tails that they wrap around twigs and grasses to help them climb. Dormice make nests in hedges. They are becoming more rare in the UK. People are working hard to protect them from dying out.

Baby mammals

All mammals give birth to live babies. Mammal mothers feed their young with milk. Baby mammals are usually helpless. They are cared for by their parents in nests or **burrows**. Baby mammals usually stay with their parents for a few weeks before going out on their own.

mouse nest

DEER

red deer stag

There are six species of deer in the UK. They live in woodland. You can also see deer in large parks. Red deer are the largest in the UK. Muntjac deer are the smallest. Male deer, called stags, have **antlers**. Stags use their antlers to fight each other in mating season.

BADGERS

Badgers have strong front claws for digging tunnels. Their underground homes are called setts. Badgers are **nocturnal**. They come out at night to look for food, like worms, insects, bulbs, berries and even small mammals. They also have strong teeth for cracking the shells of nuts and seeds.

FOXES

Foxes live in almost every **habitat** in the UK. They adapt well to their surroundings and are good at finding food. They eat small mammals, insects, worms, berries and even fruit. They bury extra food to come back to later.

Mammals in cities

rats

Black rats and house mice often live and shelter inside buildings such as houses, barns or warehouses. Mice find scraps of food left by people. Rats sometimes eat food that is meant for farm animals. Foxes and badgers often live in cities. They make their homes in gardens, allotments and parks.

OTTERS

Otters are members of the weasel family. They live both on land and in water. They can swim underwater for up to four minutes! Otters catch fish in lakes, rivers and streams. They also hunt crabs, shellfish and even frogs.

WEASELS, STOATS AND POLECATS

Weasels, stoats and polecats look similar, although polecats are the largest of the three. Weasels are the smallest. They hunt in the daytime and eat small mammals. Some stoats in the north of the UK turn white in the winter to camouflage themselves in the snow. Polecats **raid** birds' nests for eggs to eat.

polecat

weasel

BATS

Bats have wings. They are the only mammals that can fly. They dive through the air at night to catch flies and other bugs to eat. The smallest and most common bat in the UK is the pipistrelle bat. Baby pipistrelles are tiny and hairless. They drink their mother's milk until they can fly and hunt for themselves.

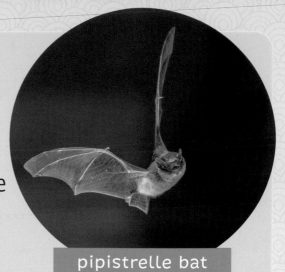
pipistrelle bat

Mammals in the sea

grey seal

SEALS

Common seals and grey seals live around Britain's coasts. In the autumn, females gather on beaches to give birth. Seals have a thick layer of **blubber** under their skin to keep them warm in cold seas. Their flippers help them to swim and hunt for fish.

DOLPHINS AND WHALES

Dolphins and whales are mammals. Minke, pilot, sperm and humpback whales can sometimes be seen in Scotland. Bottlenose dolphins can be seen off the Welsh and Cornish coasts.

bottlenose dolphin

Reptiles

Reptiles are cold-blooded. They are covered in scales. There are two main types of reptiles that live in Britain: snakes and lizards. Sea turtles also visit British shores. Reptiles are usually very fast and shy animals, so you need to be quick to spot them!

Snakes

Snakes are **carnivores**. They can't chew, so they swallow their food whole. Snakes, such as the barred grass snake, do not have eyelids. They have forked tongues. These tongues are special. They are used for smelling rather than tasting! Snakes flick their tongues to collect different smells from the air.

GRASS SNAKES

There are three species of snakes in the UK. Grass snakes are the largest. They are greenish in colour, with black patches. Females lay eggs in warm, rotting plants and leaves. Grass snakes are often found near water. They can swim well.

ADDERS

Adders are grey or brown with a zigzag pattern on their backs. They are the only venomous snake in Britain. When an adder bites its **prey**, it injects **venom** through sharp teeth called fangs. Adders hunt lizards, small mammals and some birds.

SMOOTH SNAKES

Smooth snakes are rare. They have smooth, shiny scales. Smooth snakes like to live in sandy places.

How do reptiles grow?

Most reptiles lay eggs. Reptile mothers usually bury their eggs underground. The eggs hatch and baby reptiles come out. Reptiles get bigger and stronger as they grow. The adder does not lay eggs. It gives birth to live young.

grass snake eggs

grass snake young hatching

adult grass snake

Lizards

Lizards are also reptiles. Unlike snakes, they have eyelids. Most lizards have legs and are good climbers. They mostly eat insects. They like to hide under rocks or in small holes in the ground. You might see lizards **basking** in the sun to warm up.

SAND LIZARDS

Sand lizards live near beaches and on **sand dunes**. They are the only egg-laying lizards in the UK. They lay their eggs in the sand. The baby lizards are about 6 centimetres long when they hatch.

COMMON LIZARDS

This is the UK's most common reptile. It lives in many different **habitats**, from woodland to grasslands.

SLOW WORMS

Slow worms look like snakes but they are legless lizards. Females keep their eggs inside their bodies until they are ready to hatch. The young are born still inside their eggs. Then they hatch out.

Turtles

Turtles live in the sea. They have shells on their backs for protection. Turtles are a rare sight in the UK. They do not live here all year round. Sometimes leatherback turtles can be spotted around our coasts.

LEATHERBACK TURTLES

Leatherbacks can be huge, up to 2 metres long. Their shells are leathery and softer than most turtles. They migrate 7,000 kilometres each year. They spend time around Britain on their journeys because of the warm seas and the swarms of jellyfish that they eat.

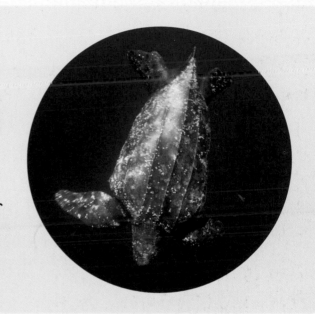

What are warm-blooded and cold-blooded animals?

Mammals and birds are warm-blooded. They can make their own body heat, even when it is cold outside. Most reptiles, amphibians and fish are cold-blooded. They cannot make their own body heat. They need to lie or swim in the sun to get warm. If they get too hot, they hide in the shade to cool down.

Amphibians

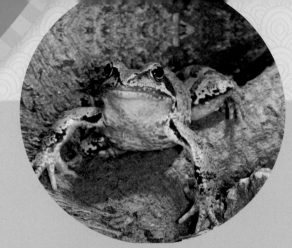

Amphibians spend their lives in the water and on land. Adult amphibians have **lungs** but they mainly breathe through their skin. Amphibians often **hibernate** in the winter. They bury themselves in mud at the bottom of lakes and ponds. They also hide in logs and under rocks or leaves. All amphibians live alone. They only spend time with other amphibians when they **mate**. Frogs, toads and newts are amphibians.

Frogs

Frogs have long and strong hind legs. They help them to swim fast through water and leap away from **predators**. Frogs use their front legs to pull themselves through plants and weeds that grow near water. Their webbed feet act like flippers and help them to swim faster.

COMMON FROGS

Common frogs are usually dark green or brown. They can have spots or stripes. They live in damp places all over the UK, close to fresh water for **breeding**.

BRITISH POOL FROGS

These are very rare frogs. They are smaller than common frogs. They often have a yellow stripe along their backs.

Toads

Toads have dry bumpy warts on their backs. The warts have a special job. When a predator attacks, the warts release a nasty-tasting poison.

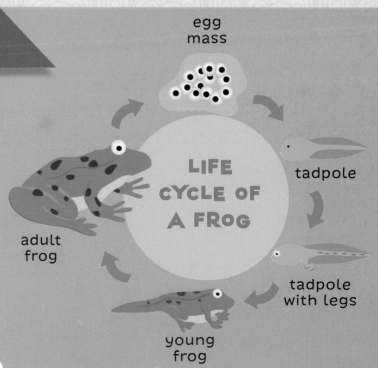

COMMON TOAD

Common toads have bumpy brown and grey skin. They walk or hop. You might see a toad in your garden, especially if there is a pond nearby!

NATTERJACK TOAD

Natterjack toads are rare in the UK. They run rather than walk or hop. They live in sandy places near warm water for breeding. Unlike other amphibians, natterjack toads don't mind salty water. They often spend time in shallow pools near the sea.

Amphibian babies

Frogs, toads and newts lay their eggs in fresh water, such as ponds. Frogs' and toads' eggs are called spawn. Newts lay individual eggs and wrap them in the leaves of water plants. Frog and toad babies are called tadpoles. They live in the water when they first hatch. They breathe through **gills**. After several weeks tadpoles grow legs and lungs and move on to land.

LIFE CYCLE OF A FROG

egg mass

tadpole

tadpole with legs

young frog

adult frog

Newts

Newts have long tails. Like frogs and toads, newts like to live in damp places near fresh water. They eat worms, small fish, snails and insects. They even eat tadpoles!

GREAT CRESTED NEWT

When it is time to breed, the male great crested newt grows a white flash on its tail. The female grows an orange flash. Great crested newts are **endangered** and protected. You must not touch them if you see them.

PALMATE NEWT

Palmate newts are the smallest in the UK. Males grow a low, smooth crest on their backs when they are ready to **mate**. Females lay their eggs in spring. By summer, baby newts have grown legs and move on to land.

SMOOTH NEWT

These are the most common newts in the UK. The males have a bigger crest than the palmate newt. Smooth newts are nocturnal. They hide under rocks during the day.

Fish

dorsal fin

tail fin

pectoral fin

The British Isles are surrounded by water. There are thousands of different fish swimming in our seas. Freshwater fish live in lakes, ponds, rivers and streams. Fish live and breathe in water.

They breathe through **gills** on each side of their head. They absorb water and oxygen through the gills. Most fish are covered in scales. They have fins to help them swim.

How do fish grow?

All fish grow in eggs with soft shells. Larvae are the tiny young. They hatch from the eggs and eat the egg yolk. They grow into fry, or small fish, and can feed themselves. Fry get bigger and stronger as they grow into adult fish.

egg

fry

adult fish

Freshwater fish

Fresh water is not salty. It is found in lakes, ponds, rivers and streams. Many fish spend all or some of their lives in fresh water.

SALMON

Salmon can grow over a metre in length. They spend a lot of time at sea, but come to fresh water to **breed**. They travel **upstream** in the summer. Sometimes you can see salmon leaping up waterfalls on their journeys. Females make little dips in the river bed and lay their eggs there. The young fish stay in the river for up to six years. Then they travel to the sea.

TROUT

Trout have sharp teeth on the roof of their mouth. They use them to hunt and eat small fish and flying insects.

Swim bladder

Fish can float underwater because they have a swim bladder. Swim bladders look a bit like tiny bags. They fill with air. This stops the fish from sinking.

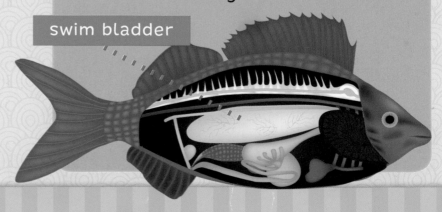

swim bladder

EELS

Eels are long, narrow fish. They are smooth, not scaly like most fish. Eels leave freshwater rivers to breed at sea. The babies, called elvers, return to fresh water to grow.

MINNOWS

Minnows are very small fish. A **shoal** is a large group of fish that swims together. By swimming in a shoal minnows have a better chance of staying safe.

PIKE

Pike are large fish. They hide among weeds in slow-moving rivers and lakes. They can burst up to the surface of the water to grab fish, frogs or even ducklings!

BREAM

Bottom-feeders are fish that eat food from the sea or river floor. Bream stir up the mud at the bottom of rivers and canals. They are searching for their favourite types of food – insects, snails and worms!

Sea fish

ROCK GOBY

The rock goby lives in rockpools and shallow rocky seas. Its pectoral fins are like suckers. It uses them to attach itself to rocks. This stops it being washed away by waves.

SHARKS

Did you know there are sharks in Britain? Some sharks spotted in our seas include the Mako shark and the basking shark. Basking sharks come to Britain in the summer. They are the second largest fish in our seas. They have huge mouths, which they keep open. They feed on **plankton**.

basking shark

FLOUNDERS

Flounders are flatfish found around the UK. They have eyes on one side of their head. They spend time on the seabed.

MACKEREL

Mackerel are slim fish that can swim fast. They have dark tiger stripes on their bodies.

SEAHORSES

Seahorses look like tiny swimming horses. But they are actually a type of fish! Seahorses eat plankton and shrimp. They suck up food through their long snouts.

Other animals in the sea

As well as fish, there are many other animals living in our seas. These include crabs, shellfish, jellyfish and octopuses.

CUTTLEFISH

The cuttlefish lives in deep water but comes to shallow water around the coast to **breed**. You may find cuttlebones washed up on beaches. They are the shell from inside the cuttlefish.

HERMIT CRABS

Hermit crabs can often be seen in rockpools. They have hard **pincers**. They live inside the empty shells of other animals. Their bodies are soft, so they stay inside the shell to be safe.

STARFISH

The common starfish is orange and has five arms. It eats the cockles and mussels that are attached to rocks in and near the sea.

Minibeasts

There are more minibeasts living in Britain than any other type of animal! Minibeasts look and act in different ways depending on how they live.

BEES

Nectar is a sweet liquid found inside flowers and plants. Honey bees collect nectar from flowers and use it to make honey.

BUTTERFLIES AND MOTHS

There are many types of butterflies and moths in the UK. Butterflies can usually be seen in the daytime. Most moths come out at night. The peacock butterfly has colourful wings. The eye spots on its wings look like the eyes of a larger animal. They scare the butterfly's **predators**.

WASPS

Wasps live in large **colonies**. They chew up wood to make paper, then use it to build their nests. Bees and wasps have stingers. Stingers inject **venom** (poison) into their enemy's skin. This leaves a painful sting.

wasp stinger up close

ANTS

Wood ants live in mounds. They build the mounds from dead leaves, pine needles and moss that they find on the forest floor.

LADYBIRDS

Ladybirds are easy to see with their red and black-spotted wing cases. Their colours tell birds and other animals that they do not taste good! Aphids are tiny bugs that nibble at plant leaves and stems. Ladybirds can eat up to 50 aphids a day!

What is an insect?

Many minibeasts are insects. Insects have six legs. They also have two **antennae** and lay eggs They do not have bones inside their bodies. Instead they have an **exoskeleton**, which is like a hard shell around their bodies for protection. Insects' bodies have three parts: the head, the thorax and the abdomen.

thorax

wasp

head

abdomen

BEETLES

There are many types of beetles. The male stag beetle has huge horns. It uses them to fight other beetles at **mating** time.

male stag beetle

GRASSHOPPERS

Grasshoppers and crickets can often be found in open grassy areas in the summer. Male grasshoppers rub their legs against their wings. This makes a chirruping sound that attracts females. You might hear this on a sunny day.

grasshopper

DRAGONFLIES

Dragonflies and damselflies are strong fliers. They can even hover in one place. They have large eyes for spotting **prey**.

dragonfly

WATER BOATMAN

This brown bug lives in ponds and lakes. It has long back legs. It uses them like paddles to swim. The water boatman swims upside down on the surface of the water.

How do minibeasts grow?

Some minibeasts change form as they grow. This is called metamorphosis. Caterpillars hatch from eggs. When they are grown, caterpillars form a pupa, or chrysalis. Inside the chrysalis they turn into butterflies. An adult butterfly emerges from the chrysalis.

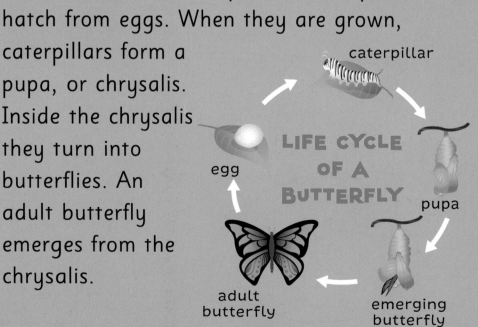

LIFE CYCLE OF A BUTTERFLY

caterpillar

egg

pupa

adult butterfly

emerging butterfly

Other minibeasts

Not all minibeasts are insects. Here are some common creepy crawlies that are not insects.

WORMS

Earthworms are long, legless minibeasts. They feed on decaying plants in the soil. Gardeners like worms because they keep the soil in good condition for growing plants.

earthworm

SPIDERS

There are around 650 types of spider in Britain. Spiders have eight legs. The common house spider lives in dark corners in people's homes and garages. Spiders have special hairs all over their bodies. These hairs help the spider to hear when a prey animal is moving near by.

SLUGS AND SNAILS

Slugs and snails have two pairs of tentacles, one big and one small. They have eyes on the tips of the big tentacles. They use the small pair for smelling things. Snails have hard shells. They can hide inside the shell. Slugs have no shells.

snail

slug

Glossary

antenna feeler on the head of an animal

antler horn on an adult (usually male) deer

backbone part of the skeleton that goes from the head to the tail

bask to lie in the sun

blubber thick layer of fat found on some sea mammals

breed when males and females join together to produce young

burrow nest or home, usually underground

carnivore animal that eats only meat

colony big group of animals all living together

endangered in danger of dying out

exoskeleton tough, outer coat or shell of invertebrates such as insects or crabs. It protects and supports their soft bodies.

gill part of a fish's or young amphibian's body used for breathing in oxygen from water

habitat particular place where plants and animals live

hibernate to go into a deep sleep-like state for winter

lung part of the body used for breathing oxygen from the air

mate when a male and female come together to make babies

nocturnal animal that sleeps in the day and comes out at night

pincer claw

plankton tiny animals and plants that live in the sea

predator animal that hunts and eats other animals

prey animals that are hunted and killed for food

raid attack a place, usually to steal something

sand dunes mounds or small hills of sand, usually on the coast

shoal big group of fish

stun knock out

thrive live well

upstream the direction of a river towards its beginning

venom poison

Find out more

BOOKS

Naturetrail Book of the Countryside, Brin Edwards (Usborne, 2013)

Show Me Insects, Mari Schuh (Raintree, 2018)

Show Me Reptiles, Megan Cooley Peterson (Raintree, 2018)

Wild Animals (Collins Gem), John A. Burton (Collins, 2009)

WEBSITES

www.bbc.co.uk/nature/places/United_Kingdom
Visit this website to learn about many other types of British animals.

www.forestry.gov.uk/wildwoods
Discover more British mammals, minibeasts and reptiles at this website.

Index